Energy Alternatives

Look for these and other books in the Lucent
Overview series:

Acid Rain
AIDS
Animal Rights
The Beginning of Writing
Dealing with Death
Drugs and Sports
Drug Trafficking
Endangered Species
Garbage
Homeless Children
The Olympic Games
Population
Smoking
Soviet-American Relations
Special Effects in the Movies
Teen Alcoholism
The UFO Challenge
Vietnam

Energy Alternatives

by Barbara Keeler

LUCENT
B·O·O·K·S

LUCENT Overview Series   OUR ENDANGERED PLANET

OUR ENDANGERED PLANET

Library of Congress Cataloging-in-Publication Data

Keeler, Barbara.
    Energy alternatives / by Barbara Keeler.
        p.   cm. — (Lucent overview series)
    Includes bibliographical references and index.
    Summary: Discusses the present energy crisis, types of fuels now
in use, alternative energy sources, and the conservation of energy.
    ISBN 1-56006-118-9
    1. Renewable energy sources—Juvenile literature.   [1. Renewable
energy sources.]   I. Title.   II. Series.
TJ808.2.K44   1990
333.79'4—dc2   90-40172
                                                              CIP
                                                               AC

*To my husband, Don Keeler, whose contributions
made this book possible, and our daughter, Joanne Norbut,
who shares our concern for our endangered planet.*

Acknowledgments

The author wants to thank all the individuals and organizations whose time and expertise contributed to this book.

American Academy of Sciences, especially Roger Billings and Janis Carre; California Energy Commission, especially Robert Aldridge, B. B. Blevins, Greg Newhouse, and Nan Powers; Chevron, U.S.A. Inc.; El Segundo Library, especially Karen Stone and Cindi Pickens; Energy Information Administration, especially William Jeffers; General Motors; Los Angeles Department of Water and Power; Southern California Edison; United States Department of Energy, especially Betsy O'Brien, Jack Cadogan, John Carlin, Craig Cranston, Robert Dietrich, Edward J. Flynn, Joan Heinkel, Susan Shaw, Scott Sitzer, and Bill Trapman; Windstar Foundation

Contents

Introduction

IN THE TWENTIETH CENTURY, people depend on unlimited energy to power their everyday lives. Consider the number of energy-run devices and conveniences people use in the course of an average day. Millions of people awaken to the alarm from their electric clocks or clock radios. If the morning is chilly, people switch on their electric blankets or turn up the dial of the thermostat for heat. Entering the bathroom, people take for granted that twisting a knob will produce a warm shower and that flipping switches will activate electric razors, toothbrushes, hair driers, and curling irons.

In the kitchen, many devices are needed to prepare the average breakfast. Cold milk, cream, and juice come out of the refrigerator. From toasters, stoves, and microwaves come hot toast, eggs, bacon, and coffee. After eating, people load the dirty dishes into an electric dishwasher.

Leaving the house, people rely on cars, buses, trains, and other modes of energy-driven transportation to get to work or school. The factories, offices, and schools are lit, heated, and air-conditioned by energy produced in nearby power stations. In offices and schools, typewriters, computers, intercoms, and dozens of other devices work on electricity. On the roads, trucks carry goods from town to town, while up above, airplanes transport people and mail from state to state and country to country.

(opposite page) Energy powers everything from common household appliances to the computer-controlled robots used at this Chrysler Corporation automobile assembly plant.

9

In the United States, people depend heavily on cars for getting to and from work and running errands.

At the end of the day, energy powers the devices people use for relaxation and entertainment. Televisions and radios bring comedy and drama into people's living rooms. Record, tape, and compact disc players reproduce music from recording studios and concert halls.

Without abundant energy, none of the devices and conveniences mentioned would work. All the inventions that people take for granted would be useless. Human beings would have to live as their primitive ancestors did. They would have to travel by foot or horse, produce light and heat using fire, and entertain themselves by telling stories. While it might seem that we may never be in danger of living without these conveniences, the fact is that many supplies of energy are quickly running out. Scientists in many countries are constantly searching for new sources of power to keep civilization running smoothly. Whether people in the future will continue to enjoy the benefits of abundant energy will depend on the success of this search for new energy sources.

1

Energy from Fossil Fuels

MOST OF THE ENERGY used to power modern civilization comes from three fuels—oil (or petroleum), coal, and natural gas. People began using these fuels thousands of years ago and became increasingly reliant on them as time went on. By the twentieth century, humanity was almost totally dependent on fossil fuels for energy production.

Fossil fuels formed millions of years ago when prehistoric plants and animals lived and died on the land and in the seas. As the dead plants and animals decomposed, or decayed, their remains often settled on the bottoms of lakes and oceans. There, layers of mud, clay, and sand slowly covered the remnants. Over the course of millions of years, the layers grew thicker, and the great weight and pressure caused the once-living materials to change into oil, coal, and gas. Since scientists call the remains of prehistoric plants and animals fossils, people came to call substances formed in this manner fossil fuels.

Early uses of coal

The first fossil fuel used to produce energy was coal. The ancient Romans heated their homes with it more than two thousand years ago. Later, people in

(opposite page) Petroleum, one of three widely used fossil fuels, must be distilled at refineries before it can be used.

13

many parts of Europe used the substance not only to heat their homes but also to heat and soften metal in blacksmiths' workshops. People also learned to make mortar from coal heated limestone.

In the early 1700s, metal industries in England began using coal in iron production and later, in the making of steel. Along with the invention of the coal-powered steam engine, these processes helped transform Europe and the United States into industrial societies in the 1700s and 1800s. This great transformation into an age of machines is referred to as the Industrial Revolution. During these years, coal provided power for trains, large ships, and steam engines in factories. When electricity came into general use in the late 1800s, much of it was generated by burning coal.

Coal use in modern times

Modern societies still use coal to produce electricity. Coal-run power plants generate electricity by burning coal to heat water. The water turns to steam, which then creates mechanical energy, the energy of motion, by spinning the blades of a turbine. The turbine is connected to an electrical generator, or dynamo, which converts the mechanical energy into electricity. In 1988, coal-run electricity plants in the United States burned over 750 million tons of coal

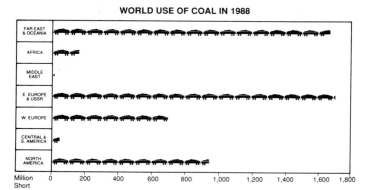

WORLD USE OF COAL IN 1988

Source: Energy Information Administration/*International Energy Annual 1988*

and generated 57 percent of the country's electricity. An average coal-burning electricity plant produces 230 megawatts of electricity. This is enough to provide a city of 100,000 people, about the size of Reno, Nevada, with all of its power.

In 1990, the total amount of coal burned in the United States for electricity, heat, and machine power reached 900 million tons per year. According to the United States Energy Information Administration, that figure will reach almost 1.5 billion tons by the year 2010. Fortunately, even at this high rate of consumption, there will still be some coal left because the United States has more coal resources than any other county. Experts estimate that four trillion tons of coal exist within U.S. borders. It might seem, therefore, that there is enough coal to supply the

Coal-powered steam engines helped transform Europe and the United States into industrial societies.

Strip mining for coal has scarred this Wyoming landscape, but brought prosperity to the state's economy.

country with energy for at least several hundred years. But although coal is plentiful, it has some serious drawbacks.

Drawbacks of coal

The chief disadvantage of coal is that it is difficult, dangerous, and expensive to mine. Some coal exists near the earth's surface and is collected by strip mining, a process that relies on explosives to break up the ground. Huge steam shovels then remove the entire surface of the land, including grass, trees, and brush. However, most coal exists in underground layers called seams, ranging in thickness from one inch to more than one hundred feet. Extracting underground coal requires that miners tunnel hundreds and sometimes thousands of feet into the earth. Cave-ins and floods from underground streams are common in such tunnels. Explosions due to sparks igniting coal dust are also frequent hazards. Mine safety equipment is expensive, including de-

Hundreds of acres of prime agricultural land in Illinois have been strip mined for coal.

vices that protect the miners from breathing in coal dust. For centuries, coal miners have suffered from black lung disease, a fatal lung condition caused by inhaling coal dust and fumes.

As people tunnel deeper and deeper for coal, reaching and removing the substance becomes increasingly more difficult and dangerous. Entirely new coal-mining technologies will be needed to reach the deepest coal seams. Most experts say it is unlikely that such technologies will be invented in the near future. Therefore, large portions of the world's known coal deposits will eventually become impossible to mine. Like oil and gas, limited supplies of nonrenewable coal will run out sooner or later.

Even if the world had unlimited supplies of coal that were easy to mine and transport, its use would

These West Virginia coal miners must tunnel hundreds and sometimes thousands of feet into the earth to find supplies of coal. Their work is often difficult and dangerous.

still present a problem. Certain varieties of coal contain high amounts of sulphur. When burned, high-sulphur coals cause so much air pollution that many states have passed laws against burning it. Burning even the cleanest coal fouls the air much more than does burning oil or natural gas.

Although industrialized societies like the United States rely heavily on coal for energy production, they also rely on other fossil fuels. For instance, consider how, over the course of centuries, people have become increasingly dependent on oil for generating power.

Oil use by ancient peoples

People knew about oil as well as coal in ancient times. The Romans called coal bitumin and used it to caulk seams in the hulls of their ships. The Greek

The Chinese began extracting oil from the ground in the 1200s using techniques now considered primitive. Oil drilling and refining techniques have progressed substantially, as this modern oil refinery shows.

In cities around the world, a driver pumping gasoline into his or her car is a common sight.

general Alexander the Great and other ancient commanders used barriers of burning oil to halt the advance of enemy troops.

Most of the oil used by the ancients came from small pools that formed by slow, natural seepage from beneath the earth. People needed and wanted larger sources of oil. But unlike coal, which often existed near the surface of the ground, large oil deposits were usually deeper and harder to extract. The Chinese found this out in the 1200s when they drilled into the earth looking for salt. Below the salt deposits, at a depth of more than two thousand feet, they found pockets of oil. Although they managed to extract small amounts of oil, their equipment was not designed to remove this product, and they eventually gave up looking for it.

Oil in modern times

In the mid-1800s, using the more advanced machinery developed during the Industrial Revolution, people learned to drill for oil more easily. In 1859, a prospector named Edwin Drake drilled the first modern oil well in Titusville, Pennsylvania. He produced several thousand barrels of oil in his first year of operation. In 1863, only four years after Drake's strike, the United States produced almost three million barrels of oil. By the year 1900, the United States produced about sixty million barrels of oil each year, and it began to replace coal as a heating fuel.

Converted to gasoline, oil also became the fuel for the transportation vehicles of the twentieth century.

This Saudi Arabian well has produced more than twenty-two million barrels of oil since it was first drilled in 1938. It is the world's most productive oil well.

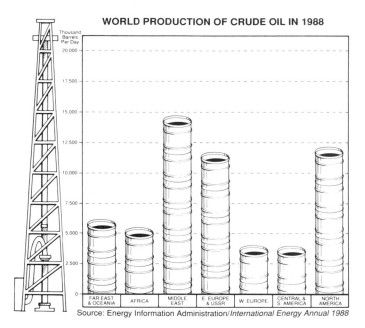

WORLD PRODUCTION OF CRUDE OIL IN 1988

Source: Energy Information Administration/*International Energy Annual 1988*

Because it is easy to store and carry, gasoline is well-suited for mobile machines, like cars and airplanes, that must take their energy sources with them. Further increases in the demand for oil came during World Wars I and II, when there was an enormous need for fuel for planes, trucks, and tanks. By the late 1940s, oil was the world's most widely used energy-producing fuel.

But people learned to use oil for more than just heating and transportation. Much of the oil consumed by modern societies is used to produce synthetic substances, manufactured materials that do not occur in nature. For instance, oil is a major component of synthetic rubber, from which tires are made. Fibers such as nylon and polyester, as well as most types of plastic, have oil bases. In addition, many companies use oil in the manufacture of pesticides, and even some medicines contain it.

With all the modern uses for oil, demand for new supplies of the substance constantly grew. So oil prospectors stepped up their searches worldwide. In

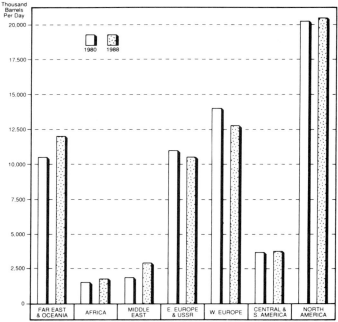

WORLD USE OF PETROLEUM IN 1980 AND 1988

Thousand
Barrels
Per Day

1980   1988

20,000

17,500

15,000

12,500

10,000

7,500

5,000

2,500

0

| FAR EAST & OCEANIA | AFRICA | MIDDLE EAST | E. EUROPE & USSR | W. EUROPE | CENTRAL & S. AMERICA | NORTH AMERICA |

Source: Energy Information Administration/*International Energy Annual 1988*

the first half of the twentieth century, major oil strikes occurred in Venezuela, Indonesia, Mexico, and the Middle East. Prospectors found the biggest deposits of oil in Middle Eastern countries like Saudi Arabia, Iran, and Kuwait. In 1964, oil engineers announced that 61 percent of the world's oil deposits existed in the Middle East. That area continues to be an important source of oil, competing with the United States, the Soviet Union, Venezuela, and other countries for major shares of the world oil market.

A great deal of oil is extracted from the earth each year. In 1990, there were 600,000 land-based oil wells, more than eight hundred ocean oil rigs, and eight hundred oil super tankers in operation worldwide. The land-based wells alone pump as much as sixty-five million barrels a day.

This high rate of pumping requires oil companies to constantly seek new oil deposits. By 1980, scientists estimated that there were about 650 billion barrels of oil in known, or proven, deposits worldwide. Since one barrel equals forty-two gallons, that amounted to more than twenty-seven trillion gallons of oil. U.S. deposits totaled about twenty-seven billion barrels, or more than a trillion gallons. Prospectors relentlessly search for new oil deposits in order to keep pace with increasing demand for fuel oil. For instance, in 1989, the United States alone burned over seventeen million barrels of oil each day.

The early oil prospectors found that most oil deposits existed alongside large pockets of natural gas,

Oil is found both on land and beneath the ocean. This oil rig is one of more than eight hundred ocean rigs operating in 1990.

Natural gas, refined in plants like this one in California, burns more cleanly than other fossil fuels.

which, like oil, could be burned as a fuel. Natural gas can produce a lot of energy when only a small amount of it is burned. Of all the fossil fuels, natural gas burns the cleanest, which means it produces the least amount of soot and other air pollutants. In addition, it is light and can be cheaply transported over long distances. Over the years, gas has proved useful in generating heat and electricity and in powering many appliances.

By 1900, the United States produced and burned hundreds of millions of cubic feet of natural gas each year. In 1989, the country used more than eighteen trillion cubic feet of gas. That amounted to 10 percent of the electricity and 22 percent of all the energy produced in the United States. Energy experts predict that yearly gas consumption will continue to rise in the 1990s.

There are about 4,000 trillion cubic feet of natural gas in proven deposits worldwide. About 10 percent of this supply exists within U.S. borders, mainly in Alaska. Prospectors continue to search for new reserves of natural gas, as well as coal and petroleum, to meet the world's constantly rising demands for energy.

The drawbacks of fossil fuels

During the twentieth century, coal, oil, and natural gas businesses grew into huge industries, supplying modern civilization with most of its power. Until the late 1960s and 1970s, most people were unaware of the serious drawbacks to using fossil fuels. Then, environmental groups and energy experts began to draw attention to these problems. The public learned that there is a price attached to enjoying abundant energy. It became clear that there might be much less available fuel and a much more polluted world in the future.

One of the most important disadvantages of fossil fuel use was perhaps the least obvious until 1973. At that time, the United States and other large industrial countries learned that they were dangerously dependent on oil for generating power.

The energy crisis of 1973

Dependence on oil did not seem like a disadvantage before 1973 because the United States had always enjoyed an abundant supply of the fuel. Until the mid-1970s, the country consumed much more oil than it produced. So it imported much of its petroleum from Middle Eastern nations like Saudi Arabia, Iran, and Kuwait. These and other oil-producing nations belonged to the Organization of Petroleum Exporting Countries (OPEC), which had shipped oil inexpensively to larger countries like the United States for decades.

Eventually, the OPEC nations grew tired of selling such an important commodity so cheaply. To show the United States how dependent it had be-

When Arab oil-producing nations cut off shipments to the United States in 1973, gasoline shortages and panic-buying led to traffic jams like the one that developed around this New York City gas station.

After the energy crisis, the United States stepped up the search for new oil deposits and pushed ahead with construction of the eight hundred mile Alaskan pipeline. Its route began at this Prudhoe Bay pump station.

come on their oil and to force oil prices to rise, they decided to cut off U.S. supplies. On October 17, 1973, the OPEC countries stopped shipping oil to the United States.

Deprived of oil from the Middle East, the United States suffered serious shortages. Gas stations ran out of gasoline, and local officials allowed people to buy gasoline on certain days of the week and in small amounts. Sometimes, as people waited for hours in lines at gas stations, the stations ran out of gasoline before all the customers had reached the pumps. The price of gasoline rose from an average of twenty-five cents a gallon to eighty cents or more a gallon. Homes and schools ran out of fuel for heat, and a few people died from the cold. Electric companies had difficulty supplying enough power to keep homes and businesses running smoothly.

Eventually, the OPEC countries resumed exporting oil to the United States, at much higher prices than before, and oil became abundant once again. But the energy crisis shocked the United States into realizing that it was much too dependent on foreign oil. To avert another such crisis, the United States stepped up its own search for new oil deposits.

The energy crisis also taught many people the importance of conserving fuel. For instance, more and more people began to buy smaller cars with better gas mileage. Also, many electric plants switched from oil fuels to natural gas and coal. And millions of homes and businesses adjusted heaters and air conditioners so that they would use less energy.

These conservation efforts were successful for a few years. Because many people conserved oil, the

The Siberian region of the Soviet Union is thought to have large, untapped oil fields. Pictured here is a Soviet oil production facility.

An oil crew drills for oil on Alaska's North Slope.

demand for the fuel did not rise much during the mid-1970s. And some individuals and companies began to explore the idea of alternative energy sources like sun and wind power.

By the late 1970s, however, as supplies of oil became plentiful once again, efforts to conserve energy and find new sources tapered off in the United States. Many people resumed buying larger, gas-greedy cars and were less careful about adjusting their heaters and other appliances. Some individuals and environmental groups began to express the concern that fossil fuel supplies might run out much sooner than anyone had anticipated.

Fossil fuels are examples of resources that, once used up, cannot be replaced or renewed. Therefore, they are called nonrenewable resources. By contrast, resources with virtually unlimited supplies, such as sunlight and wind, are called renewable. Experts like Earl T. Hayes, formerly of the U.S. Bureau of Mines, and Robert W. Baldwin, of the Gulf Oil Company, are discouraged about dwindling fossil fuel supplies. They say that at present rates of consumption, known oil and natural gas supplies will run out sometime in the twenty-first century. That means that in the span of only a few hundred years, humanity will have consumed a store of energy that nature took millions of years to create.

Mr. Baldwin and other representatives of large fuel companies admit that most of the oil that is easy to obtain is already gone. The majority of oil wells in the world produce less oil each year, and the billions of barrels remaining will be more difficult to extract than before. Some of the oil is too deep to reach using present drilling technology. And many deposits are located on the frozen arctic coast of Alaska, where drilling and transporting the oil is expensive and dangerous.

However, some energy experts, like Herman Kahn of New York's Hudson Institute, argue that this bleak scenario refers only to known supplies of oil and gas. Fuel companies continually search for and find new deposits of these substances. For example, some companies are exploring the use of oil shale and tar sands as sources of oil and gas. The experts estimate that the amount of petroleum and gas in these materials totals more than three times the oil and gas in all the known deposits in the world.

Oil from shale and tar sands

Shale, called the rock that burns by the Ute Indians, is a hard, gray rock that contains kerogen. When heated, kerogen breaks down into oil and natural gas. Unfortunately, separating oil-rich kerogen from shale is expensive and requires large amounts of energy. For this reason, large fuel companies spent rel-

A fisherman removes a dead otter from the beach as part of the cleanup effort in Alaska's Prince William Sound after the tanker Exxon Valdez *spilled millions of gallons of oil.*

atively little for exploration and development of shale energy in the 1970s and 1980s. However, fuel company spokespersons say that shale could contribute over 300,000 barrels of oil a day by the early 1900s.

Tar sands exist on sea bottoms, in deserts, and on some beaches. Like shale, tar sands contain oil that can be released through the application of heat. About two tons of tar sands are needed to produce one barrel of oil. Two Canadian companies already extract 130,000 barrels of oil a day from tar sands, supplying one-tenth of the oil Canada consumes.

But extracting oil and gas from shale and tar sands may offer only a temporary solution to the problem of dwindling fossil fuel supplies. Like known oil and gas reserves, deposits of shale and tar sands are limited. As the world's population expands and the de-

The Exxon Valdez *tries to move some of its remaining oil to a smaller ship after running aground in Prince William Sound. The spill was an environmental catastrophe.*

mand for fossil fuels increases, fuel from shale and sand will give humanity only an extra fifty- to one-hundred years' supply of energy fuel.

Conservationists complain that there is also a serious disadvantage to getting oil and gas from shale and tar sands. Mining the earth for these materials is destructive to the environment. Shale and tar sands, like coal, are usually collected by strip mining, a process that leaves behind a ravaged landscape. Although fuel companies are trying to find ways to repair strip mined countrysides, most of these areas remain barren and unusable.

Environmental problems are not exclusive to shale and tar sand extraction. All of the fossil fuels are harmful to the environment in one way or another. In addition to ruining large tracts of land by strip mining, people routinely burn and spill fossil fuels, polluting the planet's waters and atmosphere and threatening the lives and health of living creatures.

Pollution of the environment

Super tankers transport millions of gallons of oil through the world's oceans each day. Despite the safety measures taken by oil companies, tanker accidents happen frequently. By the mid-1980s, more than ten thousand accidental oil spills occurred each year worldwide. The largest spills were major disasters, fouling beaches, contaminating supplies of fresh water, and killing large numbers of fish, birds, and other animals.

For instance, the wreck of the tanker *Exxon Valdez* resulted in the worst oil spill in U.S. waters and was an environmental catastrophe for Prince William Sound on the southern coast of Alaska. On March 24, 1989, the ship slammed into Bligh Reef in the sound and spilled eleven million gallons of oil. The resulting oil slick spread over nearly three thousand square miles of ocean and fouled more than eight hundred miles of beaches. On islands more than eighty miles away from Bligh Reef, the oil hit the beaches with such force that it "sloshed up into the trees," according to witnesses. The U.S. Fish and Wildlife Service estimated that as many as 250,000 birds drowned or froze to death when oil coated their feathers. Many otters and seals also became coated with oil and died.

Luckily, fire fighting crews managed to prevent a potentially larger oil spill disaster in U.S. waters in June, 1990. An 886-foot Norwegian tanker, the *Mega Borg,* caught fire about sixty miles off the coast of Galveston, Texas. The ship burned for seven

Buildings are obscured by smog in this view of downtown Los Angeles. The city has serious air quality problems.

days, threatening to leak its cargo of thirty-eight million gallons of oil. Eventually, the fire fighters extinguished the blaze, and only a small amount of oil reached Texas beaches.

Unfortunately, every year many similar efforts to save stricken tankers fail. For example, in 1976, the 810-foot tanker *Sansinena* caught fire in Los Angeles harbor. Fire fighters could not contain the blaze, and the ship exploded, killing nine people and spilling twenty thousand gallons of oil. In that same year, more than nine thousand accidental oil leakages occurred worldwide, including spills from tankers, wells, ocean rigs, pipelines, and trucks. By 1990, the total oil spilled in the world amounted to nearly thirty million gallons each year.

Even when oil shipments safely reach their destination, the oil still ends up polluting the environment. When oil and other fossil fuels burn, they release soot, toxic chemicals, and various gases as by-products. These substances enter the atmosphere, making the air unhealthy to breathe.

Sources of pollution

Cars, trucks, and other gasoline-burning vehicles produce more than half of the world's air pollution. Much of the remainder comes from the smokestacks of coal, oil, and gas-burning factories and power stations. When air pollutants cling to water droplets in the atmosphere, the result is a cloudy mixture called smog (a combination of the words smoke and fog). In Los Angeles and other large cities, officials frequently issue smog alerts, warning people to stay indoors and avoid breathing the unhealthy air.

Another type of pollution caused by burning fossil fuels is acid deposition. This results when chemicals like sulphur dioxide and nitrogen oxide, by-products of burning fossil fuels, combine with water vapor or other particles in the air to form acids. The corrosive acids fall back to earth in rain (called

Air pollution from cars and industry in Athens, Greece is slowly eating away the marble in the ruins of ancient temples like the Parthenon. Hadrian's Arch, pictured here, also shows signs of erosion.

"acid rain"), snow, hail, mist, fog, and dew, destroying the leaves of trees and killing fish in ponds. In Athens, Greece, for example, where smog from cars and industry is particularly heavy, acid deposition is slowly eating away the marble in the ruins of ancient temples like the Parthenon. Scientists are trying to find ways of saving these ancient monuments. But they warn that if air pollution continues at present levels, acid rain and other acid deposition will eventually destroy the irreplaceable buildings. The harmful effects of acid deposition are also seen in many other parts of the world. Trees in Germany's famed Black Forest, priceless paintings in the Sistine Chapel in Italy, and the dome of the U.S. Capitol building in Washington, D.C., all suffer from deterioration due to air pollution.

Burning fossil fuels also releases large amounts of

carbon dioxide, one of several greenhouse gases that normally account for less than 1 percent of the planet's atmosphere. These gases absorb sunlight, warming the air. They are referred to as greenhouse gases because just as the glass panels of a greenhouse trap the sun's rays inside the building, carbon dioxide and methane trap these rays inside the atmosphere. Many scientists are worried that increasing levels of these gases in the air are gradually creating the greenhouse effect, or a slow global warming of

A forester points to ailing fir trees in Germany's famed Black Forest, which is suffering from the effects of acid rain.

the atmosphere. Experts, like Dr. Paul Crutzen of the Max Planck Institute in West Germany, warn that global warming could eventually cause disastrous climatic changes and partial melting of polar ice caps. This would most certainly lead to flooding of many of the world's coastlines and destruction of many major coastal cities, including New York and Miami.

Scientists, like Gerard K. O'Neill of Princeton University, and environmentalists, like Amory B. Lovins of Friends of the Earth, believe that it is time to begin replacing coal, oil, and gas as major sources of energy. They cite as reasons the disadvantages of using these substances, including society's depen-

Some scientists worry that air pollution will cause disastrous changes in climate.

dence on the fuels, vanishing supplies, and damage to the environment and climate. According to this view, if the energy demands of the future are to be met without harming the environment, existing alternative energy sources must be improved or further explored and developed. These include nuclear, water, solar, wind, and geothermal power, as well as energy from new, nonpolluting types of fuels.

2

Nuclear Energy

NUCLEAR POWER is an important alternative energy source being used worldwide to generate electricity. The first nuclear plant began operating in 1954 in the Soviet Union. By the end of 1989, there were 428 nuclear power plants operating in the world, 108 of them in the United States. In that year, U.S. plants provided about 18 percent of the country's electricity. France received about 65 percent of its electricity from nuclear plants, making it the largest producer of nuclear-generated electricity of any country.

How a nuclear plant works

Nuclear energy is produced by nuclear fission, a process in which atoms are split and energy is released. Atoms are the tiny building blocks that make up all matter. Each atom has a nucleus, or center, containing particles called protons and neutrons. Around the nucleus orbit smaller particles called electrons. Most atoms are stable, which means that they do not break apart. However, some atoms are unstable. They give off some of their particles, a process known as decay. These atoms are radioactive, and the shower of particles they give off is called radiation. Fission occurs when a particle emitted from one radioactive atom strikes the nucleus of another atom. The nucleus of the second

(opposite page) Hundreds of nuclear power plants provide nuclear energy to nations around the world.

39

atom splits, sending out one or more particles and releasing heat as a by-product.

To produce nuclear fission in a power plant reactor, scientists use a small amount of a highly radioactive element. The most common fuel element used in nuclear reactors is uranium-235. The uranium-235 is placed in long metal fuel rods, which are suspended in a tank of water. The fission process in the rods releases excess heat, which warms the water. Eventually, the water boils and gives off steam. The steam then powers a turbine, which in turn powers an electric generator. Utility cables carry the electricity from the generator directly to homes, schools, and businesses.

Power from plutonium

Nuclear reactors generate tremendous amounts of energy using relatively small amounts of uranium, a hard, silvery, metallic element. This makes uranium a

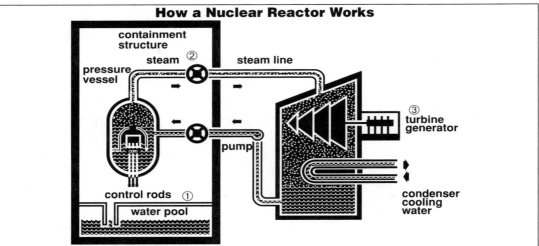

How a Nuclear Reactor Works

A nuclear reactor works just like a steam generator, except the heat used to make steam comes from nuclear fission instead of a coal furnace. The fission chain reaction occurs inside the reactor core, a large room enclosed in steel and concrete walls. Cadonium control rods keep the chain reaction from burning out of control. The heat produced by the fission heats a coolant (usually pressurized water) that runs pipes around the walls of the reactor core (1). When the coolant is hotter than 212° Fahrenheit, it is pumped to a heat exchanger until it turns to steam (2). The steam is directed to the blades of a turbine, and as the turbine turns, it generates electricity (3).

A power plant worker checks a steam-powered turbine used to generate electricity.

highly efficient fuel. Unfortunately, uranium is one of the rarest elements in nature. Only very small amounts exist in the earth's crust. Therefore, like the fossil fuels, uranium is a limited, nonrenewable resource. If the world continues to use nuclear energy as a major source of power, available stores of uranium could be exhausted in only a few decades.

One way to keep nuclear plants running without uranium is to use plutonium as a fuel. Plutonium is a radioactive element that is created as a waste product during the process of fission in a reactor core. The uranium in the fuel rods constantly emits particles and heat. In the course of a few weeks or months, most of the uranium atoms break down into atoms of other radioactive elements, and the rods are said to be spent. Some of the elements created in this way are strontium, cesium, and plutonium.

Specially designed nuclear reactors, called breeder reactors, produce large amounts of plutonium. Because the fuel they create might be used in other types of nuclear plants, breeder reactors could increase the world's reserves of nuclear fuel and make nuclear energy nearly renewable as an energy source.

Advantages of nuclear energy

The major advantage of nuclear power plants is that they efficiently produce large amounts of electricity. For instance, an average nuclear plant produces one thousand megawatts of electricity a day, enough to provide the city of Washington, D.C., with all of its power. Another advantage of nuclear plants is that they do not pollute the atmosphere as fossil fuels do. Since nothing is burned during fission, the air in and around a nuclear reactor remains free of soot, excess carbon dioxide, and other by-products of conventional fuel burning.

Still another advantage of nuclear power is that it operates using very small amounts of the earth's resources. One gram of uranium fuel produces more energy than 2.5 tons of coal or 3,840 gallons of petroleum. To supply a city of one million people

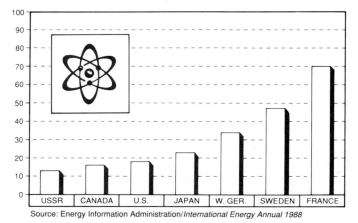

NUCLEAR POWER AS PERCENT OF TOTAL ELECTRICITY IN 1988

Source: Energy Information Administration/*International Energy Annual 1988*

with electricity, a nuclear power plant needs to burn only 3 kilograms (6.6 pounds) of fuel a day. Thus, nuclear power offers a huge energy return on a tiny resource investment.

These advantages are what originally sold utility companies and governments on the idea of investing in nuclear power in the 1950s. At that time, it appeared that electricity generated by nuclear plants was the answer to the world's energy needs. But after forty years of building and operating nuclear plants, many people have become disenchanted with nuclear power. These people, including scientists like Bruce Biewald and Donald Marron of Energy Systems Research Group in Boston, cite several serious disadvantages to generating energy through fission.

Research into fusion, such as the work done at this fusion test reactor in New Jersey, could lead to a new, safer source of energy.

Disadvantages of nuclear energy

One disappointing aspect of nuclear power is that nuclear plants turned out to be far more expensive than expected. All the plants built in the United

A dangerous nuclear accident occurred in the Soviet Union in 1986 at the Chernobyl nuclear power station, pictured here. Experts believe two explosions occurred, spewing huge amounts of radiation into the atmosphere.

States went well over their original budgets and also ended up costing more to operate than nuclear advocates anticipated. Construction costs for each of the U.S. plants finished in the 1980s averaged between three and four billion dollars. This meant that it took longer for the power companies to make a profit. These companies then charged their customers more money for electricity. In 1989, most nuclear plants sold electricity to customers for about twelve cents per kilowatt/hour. By contrast, utility companies using fossil fuels charged their customers an average of six cents per kilowatt/hour.

Another disadvantage of nuclear power is the danger of accidents. Although nuclear plants are designed so that the fission reactions cannot result in an atomic explosion, there is a danger of steam explosions from failures in the cooling systems. Such explosions can rupture the concrete shielding of the plant and allow deadly radiation to escape. Exposure to large amounts of radiation causes radiation sickness, which can be fatal. Even moderate exposure to radiation can result in cancer many years later.

Just such a nuclear accident occurred on April 26,

1986, at the Chernobyl nuclear power station in the Soviet Union. A series of errors made by plant technicians led to two huge steam explosions that shattered the reactor core and blasted off the roof of the building. As the plant burst into flames, an invisible yet deadly cloud of radiation escaped into the atmosphere.

The radioactive cloud drifted across Europe, dumping poisonous radioactive materials like cesium and strontium on soil, water, and crops. In most of Europe, radiation levels measured five to ten times normal. In some areas, the levels measured five hundred times normal.

More than 135,000 people had to be evacuated from the villages in the immediate area of the Chernobyl plant. Radiation levels in that area are still so high, Soviet officials say the people will never be able to return to their homes. Some of these people have already begun to suffer from cancer and thyroid disease because of the radiation. Even people living forty or fifty miles from the plant experienced some of the symptoms of radiation sickness, such as fatigue and loss of hair and appetite. Hundreds of deformed animals were born: eyeless pigs and calves, eight-legged colts, and animals with misshapen skulls and mouths.

Nearby European countries suffered long-term damage as well. A year after the disaster, some fish in Finland were still not fit to eat. Meat from reindeer in Lapland (northern Scandinavia) still contained more than one hundred times the radiation levels considered safe to eat. Food inspectors detected radiation in supplies of milk powder in Poland more than a year after the accident.

Soviet workers, wearing protective gear, try to isolate surrounding earth and machinery contaminated by radiation from the accident at the Chernobyl nuclear power plant.

The danger of nuclear meltdown

An even more potentially devastating type of nuclear accident is a nuclear meltdown. No such accident has yet occurred at a nuclear plant, but opponents of nuclear power worry that a meltdown might happen in the future. In a meltdown, the nuclear fuel becomes so hot, it melts through the reactor's metal and concrete protective structures. The fuel and these materials then chemically combine and get even hotter, reaching a temperature of five thousand degrees Fahrenheit. The mass of radioactive material seeps downward, eats through the floor of the reactor, and flows into the ground.

Some people used to think that such a radioactive mass would continue to eat through the earth until it emerged on the other side of the world, perhaps in China. That is how a nuclear meltdown came to be nicknamed the "China Syndrome." But scientists now realize that a meltdown would not happen that way. They believe that the extreme heat of the radioactive mass would change the materials in the soil to glass. A glass bubble would form around the mass, halting its descent.

California's Diablo Canyon Nuclear Power Plant has extra reinforcement to guard against damage that could be caused by an earthquake.

However, there would most likely be steam explosions when the hot mass encountered water in the soil. These explosions would release huge amounts of nuclear materials into the atmosphere and water table, the level below which the ground is saturated with water. A tremendous catastrophe would result, especially if the reactor was located near a populated area. In 1965, The American Atomic Energy Commission estimated that a typical meltdown would kill twenty-seven thousand people, seriously injure another seventy-three thousand, and cause seventeen billion dollars in property damages.

Proponents of nuclear power, like the American Nuclear Society in La Grange Park, Illinois, are not worried about nuclear meltdowns. They argue that a meltdown could occur only if all of the many backup safety systems in a nuclear plant failed at the same time. According to this view, a meltdown is such a remote possibility that it should not be considered a realistic disadvantage of nuclear power. Much more pressing a problem, say nuclear advocates and opponents alike, is what to do with deadly nuclear wastes.

Problems with nuclear wastes

Spent nuclear waste materials are still highly radioactive and extremely dangerous. They cannot be destroyed and must be kept away from the environment for thousands of years. By 1985, U.S. reactors alone had produced more than twelve thousand tons of nuclear wastes. Experts expect that more than seventy thousand tons will have been generated by the year 2000.

The nuclear industry has tried to figure out what to do with these waste materials for years. At present, the wastes are stored in specially made metal containers that are stacked in pools of water near nuclear reactors. But, say nuclear experts, most of the pools are already overloaded. Many fear that earthquakes or floods might cause the containers to rupture and release deadly radiation into the environment.

There have been several suggestions for dealing with nuclear wastes. Says chemist Melvin D. Joesten:

> The premise is to get the wastes as far away from us as possible. Fanciful schemes, such as rocketing the nuclear waste into the Sun or deep space or burying it in the deep oceans, have been largely dismissed as too expensive and risky. The [U.S.] Department of Energy is committed to putting on-line in 1998 underground storage chambers carved in salt beds, clay, or rock.

Joesten and other scientists say that it is still unclear whether the government's plan will be an effective permanent solution.

The future of nuclear power

The problems of storing nuclear wastes, soaring building and maintenance costs, and fears of more Chernobyl-like accidents have eliminated much of the enthusiasm once shown for nuclear power. There is a growing fear that the drawbacks of nuclear plants might outweigh their benefits. This attitude has already affected some governments and large companies. For instance, no new nuclear plants were planned or ordered in the United States during the 1980s. Antinuclear activists protest the building of any new plants and demand that governments shut down existing fission reactors and find an alternative source of power.

Many scientists believe that fission plants eventually will be replaced by another form of nuclear power—fusion. Fusion is the process that powers stars like the sun. Instead of splitting atoms apart, the process of fusion joins atoms together. For example, inside a star, tremendous heat forces two atoms of hydrogen to combine, forming a heavier atom of helium and giving off energy as a by-product. This energy is the light and heat the star emits.

Fusion offers promise as a power source on earth because it will be relatively safe. It will not use or produce dangerous radioactive substances. For fuel, fusion needs only hydrogen, which is found in abundance in ordinary seawater. Another advantage of fusion is that it generates vast amounts of energy using only a tiny amount of fuel. The hydrogen contained in one gallon of water is enough to power an entire neighborhood of homes and businesses. One scientist calculated that the hydrogen in the top ten inches of Lake Superior could supply all the electricity needs of the United States for five thousand years.

Unfortunately, no one has yet figured out how to harness fusion power. Fusing atoms requires temperatures of many millions of degrees. So far, scientists have not been able to find practical ways of producing and controlling the fusion process. Very small fusion reactions have been achieved in labs, but the amount of energy expended was thousands of times higher than the amount produced. Nevertheless, nuclear scientists predict that it is only a matter of time before fusion becomes practical and replaces fission as a major source of power.

Some people say enthusiasm for nuclear power has waned because of concerns about hazards.

3

Energy from Water

THE MOVEMENT OF WATER thundering over falls and rushing furiously downriver contains abundant power. For centuries, people have harnessed the water in rivers and streams to operate mills and machines in factories. Today the power of moving water is used to generate electricity. Electricity produced in this fashion is called hydroelectric power.

Hydroelectric power plants

Hydroelectric power has several important advantages. First, compared to most methods of producing electricity, hydroelectric power is inexpensive. Also, because rain constantly replenishes rivers and streams, hydroelectric power is renewable. In addition, such power is environmentally safe, producing no water or air pollution.

The first step in building a hydroelectric power plant is to dam a river or stream and hold the water in a reservoir. The water level is much higher behind the dam than in front of it. Plant engineers allow the water from the reservoir to rush downward with terrific force, striking the blades of large turbines at the bottom of the dam. As the turbines spin, they power generators, which in turn produce electricity.

The only significant disadvantage of hydroelectric

(opposite page) Niagara Falls, the world's forty-ninth highest falls, provides hydroelectric power to eastern cities in the United States and Canada. Hydroelectric power is both inexpensive and environmentally safe.

51

Hydroelectric power requires the building of a dam to control the flow of water.

power is that plants must be located near moving water. Communities that exist far from rivers and streams can receive the electricity via large power cables, but the farther the energy is transmitted, the more expensive it becomes. For this reason, many such communities opt for electricity generated by coal or other fossil fuels.

On the other hand, communities located near swift-moving rivers and streams, especially in mountainous areas, get almost all of their electricity from hydroelectric plants. Norway, for example, one of the most mountainous countries in the world, gets more than 90 percent of its electricity from hydroelectric plants. By contrast, in 1989, only about 12 percent of the electricity used in the United States came from such plants.

Storing hydroelectric power

The most efficient and economical way to produce hydroelectric power is to keep a plant operating twenty-four hours a day. Unfortunately, the demand for power does not stay the same all day. Most homes and businesses use electrical equipment and heating and cooling systems between 7:00 A.M. and 7:00 P.M. During these hours, called peak hours, demand for electricity is usually the heaviest. At night, during off-hours, much less electricity is used. In order not to waste the power generated at night, power plant engineers store most of the electricity produced during off-hours.

At some plants, extra electricity is used to pump water back up to the reservoir. Then the same water can be used again when electricity is needed. Other surplus energy is stored in batteries. These batteries can later be used for a variety of tasks. For instance, many large companies equip their warehouses and freight yards with fleets of small electric-powered vehicles.

These companies pay hydroelectric plants for the electricity to charge the batteries of these vehicles. Since the companies usually use the vehicles only in the daytime, they conveniently charge the batteries at night. The companies find that they can run these vehicles less expensively with electricity than with fossil fuels. Another advantage is that the electric-powered vehicles do not pollute the air as gasoline-run vehicles do.

Another way off-hour hydroelectric power can be utilized is in the separation of hydrogen from water, a process called electrolysis. Water is made up of hydrogen and oxygen. Passing an electric current through the water causes the bond between the two elements to break, and each is collected for various uses. The oxygen is often used to fill oxygen tanks for airplanes, hospitals, and rescue vehicles. The hydrogen can be used as a powerful, clean-burning fuel in factories and power plants.

The future of hydroelectric power

Experts expect hydroelectric power to continue to supply mountainous countries like Norway and Switzerland with most of their electricity for generations to come. However, in countries that rely more heavily on other forms of energy, the future of hydroelectric power is more uncertain.

For instance, in the United States, due to licensing problems, hydroelectric power could enter a period of decline in the 1990s. These power plants are licensed by the government for fifty years. In the 1990s, a large number of the country's hydroelectric plant licenses will expire. Before plant owners can renew their licenses, they must deal with complaints

Many large companies use small electric-powered vehicles, such as this electric mail delivery truck used in California, because they are inexpensive to run.

HYDROELECTRIC POWER AS PERCENT OF TOTAL ELECTRICITY IN 1988

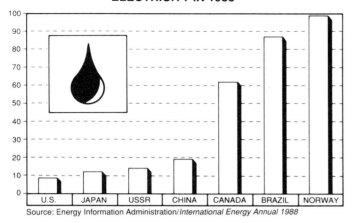

Source: Energy Information Administration/*International Energy Annual 1988*

being made by environmental groups about plant operations.

The groups charge that when dams are used to contain water in reservoirs, fish become trapped and cannot swim downstream to breed. The environmentalists want the government to deny new licenses to plant owners that refuse to make expensive changes in plant operations that might allow fish to bypass the plant. The groups also want the plant owners to allow human recreational use of areas surrounding the plants. Some people fear that although such changes would be beneficial, plant owners may find them too expensive and abandon the dams rather than pay the price.

While the future of hydroelectric power in the United States remains unclear, many large companies are exploring other forms of water-generated energy. One of the most promising areas involves taking advantage of the tides.

Energy from the tides

The tides are constantly moving, and this motion represents a form of usable energy. Many centuries ago, people in Europe used the tides to power water

Waves and tides on this Northern California coastline someday could provide a source of energy. Some countries already are experimenting with using ocean tides and waves to produce electricity.

mills. Today the tides are used to generate electricity. France has an experimental tidal plant that generates 240 megawatts of electricity. Other experimental plants exist in the Soviet Union, Canada, and China. In all, there were about a dozen tidal plants in operation worldwide in 1990.

A tidal plant works by exploiting the difference between high and low tides, in a sense, letting the ocean itself do most of the work. At high tide, a large volume of water is trapped in containers. Later, at low tide, engineers release the water, which flows back toward the sea. On its way, the water passes through the power plant, and turns turbines and generators, thus producing electricity.

One obvious advantage of tidal plants is that there are many places around the world where tides rise high enough to make building such plants feasible. Another advantage of tidal power is that it is completely renewable. Also, it does not pollute the water or atmosphere. Although tidal plants are expensive to build, advocates say they are less expensive than nuclear plants. And, once a tidal plant is built, the cost of operation is about the same as most other power plants.

One disadvantage of tidal plants is that they can be built only on ocean coastlines, making them useless to communities located far from the sea. However, proponents of tidal power point out that hundreds of millions of people worldwide live on these coastlines. They argue that these populations would benefit from any clean, renewable energy source available.

Coastal populations might also benefit from another form of power from the oceans—the energy of waves.

Wave energy

Ocean waves, like the tides, are constantly in motion and offer a source of renewable and almost limitless energy. So far, little money has been spent on research in this area, mainly because the equipment required is very expensive.

Scientists and engineers have designed about a dozen systems for generating electricity from waves. Most of these systems call for placing large turbines near the surface of the ocean. There, constant wave action would turn the blades of the turbines, which would be connected to electricity generators on nearby coastlines.

A few wave-powered generators are actually in use. For instance, one small station in Norway generates five hundred kilowatts of power. In Japan, where most of the country's large population lives near the sea, several huge wave-powered generators will be built in the 1990s. Wave power advocates say that a significant portion of the electricity used by humanity in the twenty-first century will come from ocean wave turbines. These devices will offer cheap, abundant energy with no harmful side effects or other disadvantages.

4

Solar Energy

SOLAR ENERGY is the energy of sunlight. Sunlight is a renewable resource that will exist for as long as the sun itself exists, at least several billion years. Sunlight does not pollute the environment in any way. Also, the amount of sunlight available at any given time is immense. The solar energy that reaches the ground in one hour equals the combined energies of all the fuels used by humanity in an entire year. For these reasons, solar power holds great promise for the future of human energy production.

The limits and early uses of solar power

With so much sunlight striking the earth each day, it might seem that people would need no other energy sources. However, the sunlight that reaches the earth is very spread out. Another way of putting it is that the energy of ordinary sunlight is not concentrated enough to generate much power. And tasks like operating machinery and generating electricity require a great deal of power.

For years, scientists have tried to invent ways of collecting and concentrating sunlight. More than two thousand years ago, the Greek inventor Archimedes is said to have built a huge lens. With this device, he supposedly focused the sun's rays into a white-hot beam and set afire a fleet of attacking Roman ships. Whether Archimedes actually accomplished this

(opposite page) Solar panels, like the ones installed on the roof of this California apartment complex, collect heat from the sun for warming water.

feat, people in ancient and medieval times were well aware that curved, shiny surfaces reflected sunlight to a central, very hot spot. As early as A.D. 1000, Arab scientists used such reflectors to burn wood and cook food. And in the 1700s, factories in England and other parts of Europe used large solar reflectors to melt metal in furnaces.

Modern solar collection systems

Today's solar reflectors are similar in principle to those of the past. They attempt to concentrate sunlight into a small hot beam. The advantage of modern versions is the availability of more advanced technology. Most systems use either curved or flat mirrors, which focus the solar rays onto tubes filled with water. The sunlight heats the water to temperatures of 150 degrees or more, suitable for conventional uses like showers and dishwashers. The hot water can also be used in forced-hot-water plumbing systems to heat homes, schools, and businesses.

In many parts of the world, rooftop solar collec-

With solar water heating, sunlight heats water to about 150 degrees Fahrenheit, which is warm enough for the residents of this house to shower and wash dishes.

tion systems heat the water in a majority of homes. More than half the houses in Greece and Turkey are equipped with such systems. Israel uses solar energy to heat 65 percent of the water in residential areas. And on the island of Cyprus, 90 percent of the homes use solar power to heat water.

Many homes around the world use an even simpler type of solar collection system—passive solar power. Passive systems use no reflectors or other special equipment. Instead, they rely on a home's basic design features to collect and utilize sunlight. For instance, large windows facing south can catch the sun's rays and direct them to walls composed of materials that readily absorb heat. As the walls later radiate the heat, air ducts and fans can circulate the warm air. Similarly, a concrete floor exposed to direct sunlight becomes a heat "sink," absorbing solar radiation during the day. At night, the concrete slowly releases the heat, warming the house. Passive solar systems can either be built into new homes or added to existing homes.

With more than eighteen hundred mirrors, this solar thermal power plant near Barstow, California focused sunlight on a tank of water. The water boiled and produced steam, which was used to run a turbine that generated electricity.

Solar power has proved to be useful in heating individual buildings because the systems needed are simple and inexpensive. Large-scale solar energy systems also show great promise, but they are much more expensive to build and operate.

Solar power plants

Large solar plants are still in the experimental stages in various parts of the world. In Odeillo, France, an experimental solar station uses an array of reflectors connected to timers. The timers allow the reflectors to follow the movement of the sun all day, ensuring the collection of as many solar rays as possible. The energy collected is used to power a solar "furnace," which smelts (melts) various metals for industrial purposes. The station has generated temperatures as high as sixty-three hundred degrees, enough heat to melt most metals.

Solar power plants using reflectors have also been developed in the United States. At a demonstration plant near Barstow, California, more than eighteen hundred mirrors once covered more than 130 acres of desert. The mirrors of this solar "farm" focused sunlight onto a tank of water at the top of a 310-foot tower. The focused sunlight boiled the water, producing steam. The steam in turn operated a steam turbine. This plant generated ten thousand megawatts of electricity. Unfortunately, the facility was built only to test the technology and closed down in 1988.

Another type of solar collection farm generates power using solar "ponds." These are shallow pools of water whose bottoms have been coated with a dark material that absorbs sunlight. Eventually, the water heats up and powers small turbines. Israel gets some of its energy from solar ponds located near the Dead Sea. These ponds generate five megawatts of electricity a day, enough to meet the energy needs of a small town.

Solar efficiency

Nearly all the large-scale solar plants in the world remain in the experimental stage. One reason for this is that scientists have not been able to cheaply and efficiently collect enough sunlight to generate massive amounts of power. A typical solar farm requires large expanses of land covered with reflectors in order to collect enough sunlight to generate electricity. For instance, a solar farm that collects one thousand megawatts of power needs to cover an area of nearly 5,000 acres. By contrast, a nuclear plant producing the same amount of power needs to occupy only about 150 acres.

Another reason solar plants are still somewhat impractical for generating large amounts of power is that the sun shines for only half of each day. Large power plants need to operate twenty-four hours a day to meet energy demands. Also, the weather is a factor. When it is cloudy, no solar energy can be collected. Scientists have found ways to store solar energy for nighttime or cloudy-day use. They use batteries and also trap the collected heat in underground water tanks and rocks. But these methods are inefficient, losing as much as one-fifth to one-half the energy collected. Until scientists solve these problems, large solar power plants will not meet a significant portion of the world's energy needs.

Solar cells

Solar experts, like solar-home architect Bruce Anderson, believe that another type of collection device, the solar cell, holds great promise for the future of solar power. Solar cells work without focusing or reflecting the sun's rays. The cells are made from crystals of silicon. One of the world's most common elements, silicon is found in ordinary rocks.

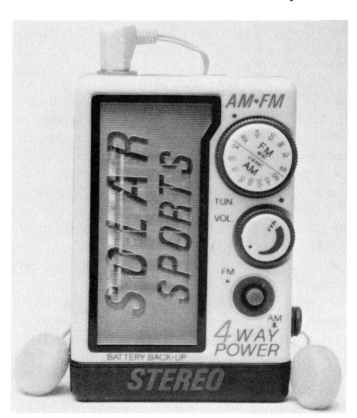

Solar cells that convert light directly into electrical energy can be used to operate radios and other small devices.

Scientists cut the silicon crystals into thin wafers, then they coat them with thin layers of metal. When sunlight strikes a solar cell, the cell converts the light directly into electrical energy. Thus, a panel of such cells can be wired to any electrical device, and the device will operate, providing the sun is shining.

Unfortunately, solar cells have the disadvantage of converting only about 15 percent of the energy in sunlight to electricity. The other 85 percent is wasted. Thus, an individual solar cell generates very little power. This means that in order to meet most energy demands, panels of solar cells must contain hundreds and sometimes thousands of individual cells. To provide all the energy needed by an average modern household, for instance, about eight hundred square feet of solar cells are required. To power entire factories and towns, solar cell panels would have to contain millions of cells and cover several square miles. Obviously, this would be a highly expensive and impractical proposition.

Expansion of solar cell use

Most solar cell systems in the United States generate between two hundred and fifty thousand kilowatts of electricity. By comparison, a typical coal or nuclear plant generates in excess of one million kilowatts. But energy experts say that improvements in solar cell technology will eventually make the cells much more efficient and economical. They point out that between 1976 and 1988, the cost of an average solar cell dropped from $44 to $5.25. And researchers are working on ways to stack the cells, hoping to increase cell efficiency from 15 to 40 percent or more.

For the moment, electricity generated by solar cells remains small-scale. Panels of cells provide power for some telephone booths, lighthouses, and scientific research stations. Since 1982, a 350-kilowatt plant using solar cells has been providing

Cloudy skies block the ability to collect energy from the sun, limiting use of solar energy in many regions of the world.

power to small remote villages in Saudi Arabia. And in a number of countries, some homes use panels of solar cells as a supplemental backup to conventional electrical systems.

Scientists believe that solar cells eventually will be used on a much larger scale. The most ambitious suggestion made so far is for the transmission of solar energy to earth from space.

Solar-powered satellites

Orbiting satellites that would collect solar energy and send it to earth were originally devised in the early 1970s. Scientists at the National Aeronautics and Space Administration (NASA) designed such satellites after solar cells had successfully been used to power ordinary satellites in the 1960s. Solar-powered satellites will collect sunlight, convert it to microwaves or laser beams, then transmit it to receivers on earth. The receivers will convert the energy directly into electricity to power entire cities. If enough of these devices are put into orbit, they will supply all the electricity needed by humanity.

Of course, to generate such massive amounts of power, solar-powered satellites will require huge ar-

Solar cells, similar to these, were used in the 1960s to power satellites. Eventually, they may be used to power orbiting satellites that will collect solar energy and send it back to earth.

rays of solar cells. A typical panel will cover several square miles. But because the panels will be in space, they will not interfere with activities on the earth's surface. Another advantage of the satellites is that they can be positioned in special orbits where they constantly face the sun. Thus, they will not be restricted by the earthly cycle of day and night, and no energy will need to be stored for later use. Also, no clouds or other weather phenomena will interfere with the operation of the satellites.

The main disadvantage of solar-powered satellites is their great expense. Building and orbiting just one such device would cost several billion dollars. For this reason, governments and large companies have been reluctant to begin building the satellites.

The future of solar power

In addition to solar-powered satellites, scientists have many other ideas for harnessing the power of the sun. One suggested device is a solar "chimney," a tower surrounded by clear plastic sheets. The plastic will trap sunlight, heating the air inside the chimney. As the hot air rises, it will create a strong current of air that will drive a wind turbine. Inventors constantly try to perfect solar-powered water pumps, refrigerators, air conditioners, battery chargers, and heating systems. The inventors believe that these devices could successfully replace versions presently powered by dwindling supplies of fossil fuels.

As these and other solar devices and technologies are created, they will help realize the huge potential of sunlight for supplying people's energy needs. Each year, enough sunlight strikes the earth to provide all of humanity with power for more than eight thousand years. If scientists can learn to harness these rays efficiently and inexpensively, people will have clean, limitless energy for as long as the sun continues to shine.

5

The Power of the Wind

ENERGY GENERATED by wind offers many of the same advantages and disadvantages of solar power. The wind is a completely renewable and virtually unlimited resource. Wind power does not pollute the environment in any way. Nor does it consume any of the planet's liquid or mineral resources.

Wind was one of the first forms of energy harnessed by humans. For instance, sailors have relied on the wind to move their ships for thousands of years. Since ancient times, people in the Middle East and Europe have used windmills for pumping water and grinding grain. Some of these very old windmills still operate in places such as the Netherlands and the island of Crete. Windmills also became popular in the American colonies in the 1600s and 1700s. By the end of the nineteenth century, 6.5 million windmills existed on farms in the United States.

Modern windmills

As the price of fossil fuels, especially oil, rose in the mid-1970s, many people became concerned about dwindling supplies of these fuels. Interest in windmills and other types of wind machines was renewed, and thousands of new windmills were built

(opposite page) Windmills like this one in the Netherlands have been used since ancient times in Europe and the Middle East for pumping water and grinding grain.

in the United States and other countries.

Wind power takes advantage of the energy in the motion of the wind. That motion turns the blades of a windmill, which spin a turbine to produce electricity. The design of the wind machines used today is often very different from that of ancient windmills. Centuries ago, windmills had many blades that revolved on a shaft that was horizontal, or parallel, to the ground. These blades would be turned by wind coming from only one direction. And because they were heavy, the blades could not turn very quickly. Today's windmills have fewer, lighter blades that turn more quickly. They are stronger and more efficient generators of power than earlier versions. Also, some modern windmills, called vertical axis windmills, have blades that revolve around a vertical, instead of a horizontal, shaft.

When many wind machines are grouped together on wind "farms," they can generate enough power to operate a power plant. In the United States, some wind farms generate more than thirteen hundred megawatts of electricity a day, enough power for a

Wind farms can generate enough power to operate a power plant. In the United States, some wind farms generate enough power to supply the electricity needs for a city the size of San Francisco.

city larger than San Francisco. In Europe, many wind farms routinely generate one hundred or more megawatts of electricity a day.

Some modern wind machines can generate electricity with wind speeds of as little as 9.6 kilometers (6 miles) per hour. Others need minimum wind speeds of 20 kilometers per hour to operate. Because these machines can be damaged by extremely high winds, most of the devices are equipped with a safety feature that shuts them down when wind

This New Mexico wind turbine (right) was the first in the nation to be hooked into a community power plant. Next to it stands a traditional windmill.

speeds get too high. Some have blades that tilt at different angles to the wind, maintaining a constant speed in spite of changing wind speeds.

Of course, wind changes direction as well as speed. So, many modern windmills are mounted on rotors that turn as the wind direction shifts. One kind of windmill, the Darrieus, can operate no matter what direction the wind comes from because it has round blades that form a circle around a vertical axis.

Every year, inventors design and build bigger and more powerful wind machines. Some of the largest individual wind turbines can generate as much as three megawatts of power, enough to supply a small village with electricity. NASA scientists have designed some very advanced wind machines, such as the MOD-2. The turbine of the MOD-2 is mounted on a tower 200 feet high and the blades are 150 feet long. The MOD-2 is so large, it cannot generate power with winds of less than fourteen miles per hour. But when wind speeds increase, the device is extremely powerful and efficient. For example, at wind speeds of twenty-eight miles per hour, the MOD-2 generates twenty-five hundred kilowatts of power. Because stronger winds blow at higher altitudes, the machine's 200 foot tower exposes the blades to more powerful wind gusts. For safety, the MOD-2 automatically shuts down when wind speeds reach forty-five miles per hour.

Advantages and disadvantages of wind power

In addition to being a renewable and nonpolluting source of power, wind energy is relatively inexpensive. In areas where high winds blow nearly year-round, wind-generated electricity costs about as much as power produced by coal and petroleum plants. Another advantage of wind power is that an average wind farm can be built in only six months, much faster than nuclear plants can be built or fossil fuels can be produced.

Unfortunately, wind power also has some major disadvantages. In the first place, the wind is not a very efficient generator of electricity. The blades of a windmill can be only so wide, so they collect only 10 to 40 percent of the wind that passes the machine. This means that many wind machines are needed to make up for the energy wasted. It takes about eight thousand windmills, each with a two-hundred-kilowatt capacity, to equal the power output of one coal-fired power plant. Obviously, very large land areas are needed to accommodate so many windmills. A

Wind has the potential to supply human energy needs as well as to topple a water tower and scatter cars and trees as it did in this Texas community.

typical wind farm requires four to five times more land than a solar farm does to generate the same amount of electricity.

Another disadvantage of wind power is that wind speeds are not constant. Sometimes there is no wind at all, and wind machines cannot generate power. Other times, winds are so strong, they damage the machines. For this reason, scientists try to locate farms in areas where the wind blows at a fairly constant speed.

Potential locations for wind machines

In addition to wind speed, scientists are concerned with the number of hours per day, week, or year that the wind must blow to consistently provide energy. They know that wind machines are most efficient in areas where the wind blows constantly or nearly constantly. Good locations include open areas such as flat plains and narrow mountain passes. Some windmill designers have suggested installing wind machines all over the Great Plains in the central part of the United States. In many sections of the Great Plains, the wind blows almost continuously.

Most operating wind farms in the United States are located in California. This is mainly because the state used to provide economic incentives for wind machines. One such incentive was the offer of a tax credit, a savings on state taxes, for any company that explored new energy sources. Home owners who installed their own wind machines to supplement power from conventional utilities also received tax credits. However, in the 1980s, California eliminated home owner tax credits and also reduced such credits for businesses. This was mainly due to federal cuts in monies for research and development for renewable energy sources. This shows how the finances of federal and state governments can affect where wind farms will be located.

One possible future location for wind farms is on

giant platforms on the surface of the ocean. One advantage of such offshore farms is that sea breezes blow more than 99 percent of the time. Another advantage is that these farms would not take up large tracts of land that could be used for other purposes. At the same time, offshore wind farms would not disturb the ocean ecosystems below them. These farms would be expensive to build, but some experts say they would make the money back after only a few years of operation.

Because of the reduction in research and development of wind machines in the 1980s, many small wind power companies went out of business. As a result, fewer wind machines were built and installed in the United States in the late 1980s than in previous years. However, interest in wind and other renewable energy sources is expected to increase in the 1990s. Used in combination with solar, water, and other renewable energy sources, wind power could play an important role in the future of energy production.

6

Geothermal Energy

SEVERAL TIMES a day in Yellowstone National Park in Wyoming, a crowd of people gathers around a hole in the ground. Each time, at the expected moment, the geyser, Old Faithful, violently erupts. It shoots over ten thousand gallons of boiling water and steam more than 150 feet into the air, then abruptly subsides until its next outburst.

Geysers, like Old Faithful, are examples of geothermal features. These are pockets of water, mud, lava, and various gases located near the earth's surface that have been warmed by heat from the planet's interior. Many other geothermal features can be seen at Yellowstone Park, including hot springs in the beds of rivers, pits of boiling mud, and holes that spout clouds of steam. Similar geothermal areas exist in other parts of the world, especially volcanic areas such as Iceland, New Zealand, and the islands of Indonesia.

(opposite page) When Yellowstone National Park's famous geyser Old Faithful erupts, it shoots more than ten thousand gallons of boiling water and steam 150 feet into the air. This activity is an example of geothermal power.

Heat from the earth's center

The heat that creates geothermal features comes from the center of the earth. When the planet was very young, all of its materials were red-hot and liquid. As the earth cooled and the materials began to solidify, the outer layers of the planet hardened first. The thicker the solid layers became, the more they insulated the hot liquid layers below, and the cooling process of the interior slowed down. That is why today, even after about 4.5 billion years, the core of the earth is still liquid and extremely hot. Scientists estimate that temperatures at the center of the planet reach eleven thousand degrees Fahrenheit, hotter than the surface of the sun.

As this great heat slowly rises through thousands of miles of solid rock, the rock absorbs the warmth. So only a small amount of the heat reaches most of the planet's surface areas. However, in the earth's outer layers, there are a few weak spots that allow more of the heat from the interior to get through. The places on the surface above these weak spots are the geothermal areas like Yellowstone Park.

The vast amounts of heat that create geothermal

Naturally heated hot springs, similar to this one in Germany, have been used by humans for many centuries for relaxation, bathing, and washing clothes.

Geothermal energy is economical but can only be produced efficiently in geothermally active locations.

features represent a potential source of usable energy for humanity. In fact, the harnessing of geothermal energy is not a new idea.

Uses of geothermal energy

People have taken advantage of geothermal energy for thousands of years. Early Europeans bathed in hot springs on the Greek island of Thera as early as 1600 B.C. People washed clothes in similar springs in Italy and the Middle East in Roman times. For centuries in Iceland, one of the most active geothermal areas in the world, people have helped heat their houses by building them on the slopes of volcanoes. Modern Icelanders utilize underground steam for heating homes.

Plant engineers test steam pressure and temperature of geothermal wells at Geysers Geothermal Power Plant.

Geothermal energy is used to generate electricity. When reservoirs of hot water lie near the earth's surface, engineers build large turbines nearby. The engineers pipe steam from the hot water to the blades of the turbines, which spin, powering electricity generators. As much as 15 percent of Iceland's electricity is now generated in this fashion.

If pockets of heated water are not available, engineers can create a geothermal "well" by drilling deep into the earth until they reach hot rocks. The engineers then force water down the well. The rocks quickly heat the water and turn it into steam, which expands and moves back up to the surface. There the steam can be piped directly into homes and businesses for general heating purposes, or it can be used to generate electricity. This geothermal technique presently provides about 10 percent of the electricity used in New Zealand. Such wells produce steam for as long as twenty to thirty years, making them very cost effective. When a well runs out of heat, engineers can quickly drill a new well only a few hundred feet away.

Limitations of geothermal energy

Although power generated by geothermal energy can be extremely economical, it has some disadvantages. First, geothermal power can be efficiently produced only in special, geothermally active locations. These are usually located in remote areas, far from population centers where energy is most needed. Transporting electricity via power lines from these distant, rugged areas is difficult and expensive.

Another problem with geothermal energy involves supplies of water. Geothermal wells, like those in New Zealand, require large amounts of water to produce steam. Even when hot rocks occur within drilling distance of the earth's surface, often there is no adequate water supply nearby. In such cases, it is usually too expensive to pipe in water

Geothermal wells require large amounts of water to produce steam.

from some distant location.

One solution to this problem would be to pick out an area with plentiful water and then drill a geothermal well deep enough to reach hot rocks. Since most lakes and rivers are not located near geothermally active areas where hot rocks lie near the surface, such wells would have to be many miles deep. Engineers have managed to drill a few of these very deep wells. However, the projects were extremely expensive. Also, the drilling brought thousands of tons of pulverized rock, sludge, salts, and other waste materials to the surface. So far, no one is sure of what to do with these wastes.

Geothermal energy and the environment

Geothermal power experts, like Phil Hanson of the Boise, Idaho, Geothermal Project, argue that the wastes from drilling geothermal wells are not a major problem. They say that generating such power will not pollute the environment nearly as badly as producing electricity with fossil fuels and nuclear reactors.

Still, if large numbers of geothermal plants are built, the pollution from these facilities will have to be dealt with somehow. And constructing and operating hundreds or thousands of geothermal plants will have some of the same effects on the surface of the land as strip mining does.

The potential of geothermal energy

If the disadvantages of building and operating geothermal plants can be overcome, this form of energy has considerable potential for generating electricity. In 1989, the few geothermal plants operating worldwide generated a combined total of 4,650 megawatts each day. This is enough power to pro-

The few geothermal plants operating worldwide in 1989 generated enough power to provide electricity for a city the size of Chicago.

vide a city the size of Chicago with all of its electricity for a day. If one hundred times as many geothermal plants were built, significant amounts of fossil fuels would be saved. For example, just one megawatt of geothermal power would save as many as eight barrels of petroleum.

The key to harnessing the heat left over from the earth's creation will be the development of new drilling technologies in the coming century. New tools and methods may allow engineers to reach depths of dozens of miles or more, making geothermal wells possible at any land location. Eventually, it may be possible to drill such wells in the deepest seabeds. It is in these areas that the earth's crust is the thinnest, only ten miles thick in some places. There, red-hot rocks will be easy to reach, and water for steam production will be nearly limitless. If such technical advancements are achieved, geothermal power will serve people for as long as the earth's core remains hot, at least several hundred million years.

7

Alternative Fuels

FOSSIL FUELS continue to be the world's most common fuels for heating homes, generating electricity, and powering vehicles. However, several alternative fuels now exist. They include the waste materials of living things, certain types of alcohol, and ordinary hydrogen. Although consumption of these products is still on a small scale, scientists expect their use to expand in coming decades. Like other sources of energy, these alternative fuels have their disadvantages. But they share one major advantage over the fossil fuels—the alternative fuels are renewable. Therefore, the larger the alternative-fuel industries become, the less people will have to depend on nonrenewable fuels.

Energy from living things

Plants and animals maintain their existence by converting food, in the form of solids, liquids, and gases from the environment, into energy. Therefore, living things have a great deal of potential energy stored in their tissues. The waste materials and even the dead tissues of plants and animals also contain potential energy.

Wood is an energy-producing fuel derived from once-living trees. When people burn wood, the stored energy is released as heat. The fire also converts some of the wood into soot, various gases, and

(opposite page) Wood from trees has been the most widely used fuel throughout most of human history. Today, only about 1 percent of the energy used in the United States comes from burning wood.

Overflowing landfills sometimes pollute the environment. Elsewhere, controlled landfills, like this one in Florida, are being converted into public parks.

other by-products. Although it is only an alternative fuel today, wood was, by far, the most widely used fuel throughout most of human history. Wood fires provided people with heat and cooked food from the days of primitive hunting societies to the age of world exploration in the 1500s and 1600s. Only during the Industrial Revolution did wood begin to play a smaller role in providing humanity with usable energy.

About 1 percent of the energy used in the United States today comes from the burning of wood. In the late 1980s, wood was the major source of heat for about five million American homes, almost 6 percent of the households in the nation. Although some people still burned their wood in traditional fireplaces, more efficient wood stoves became increasingly popular in the 1970s and 1980s. Industrial sites also burn wood in large furnaces. Paper and lumber companies, for example, rely heavily on wood wastes as a source of heat energy.

Plant and animal wastes

Living things also supply energy in the form of solid, liquid, and gaseous waste materials. Examples of solid wastes are sawdust, leftover wood parts from lumber mills, leaves and wood from the forest floor, animal dung, compost made from various plants and crops, and garbage. All of these can be burned in power plants to produce electricity. Many small plants in the United States, Canada, and some European countries now regularly produce power this way.

One obvious advantage to burning animal and plant wastes for energy is that the process conveniently eliminates the problem of disposing of them. Many of these wastes end up in garbage landfills, mixed in with plastics, metals, and various toxic materials. For decades, as the population of the United States increased, garbage landfills all over the country grew larger. Eventually, overflow from these sites threatened to pollute the environment, including underground streams and reservoirs. Today more and more towns divide up their trash, separating plant and animal wastes from materials that cannot be burned for energy. The wastes are then shipped to plants that convert them into usable energy.

People also get energy from gaseous wastes. When animal dung and dead plants and animals decompose, they give off a mixture of methane and carbon dioxide. Garbage landfills and sewage treatment plants are major producers of these gases. In some experimental projects in the United States and Europe, engineers recover the gases by enclosing the landfills and sewage beds. As the gases build up within the enclosures, they are piped into storage tanks. Once collected, methane can be burned to produce electricity. One experimental plant produces fifty megawatts of electricity per day in this manner.

The major disadvantage to producing energy with waste materials is that burning them contributes to air pollution. Along with soot and carbon dioxide, the waste-burning process releases poisonous substances such as dioxin into the atmosphere. Scientists and engineers have tried to eliminate this problem in various ways. For instance, they have equipped incinerators with special filters that trap and collect soot and other solid by-products of the burning process. Also, the experts advocate separating dangerous materials from the trash before it is burned. This reduces the amount of toxic chemicals released. Many cities now require citizens to separate their own garbage and trash into different categories.

Energy from alcohol

Some liquid by-products of living things are promising alternative fuels. The two most notable examples are methanol and ethanol, both alcohols derived from wood and other plant products. These liquids make excellent fuels for power plants that produce electricity. Several alcohol-fueled power plants now operate in Brazil, where the vast rain forests of the Amazon River basin offer a large source of wood. Many people worry that Brazil will cut down the rain forests too quickly, eliminating its main source of alcohol fuel and destroying thousands of plant and animal species in the process.

The most important use for methanol and ethanol is as fuel for cars, trucks, and other vehicles. Both alcohols can be used as substitutes for gasoline or diesel fuel. Already, some car manufacturers have recognized the potential of these alternative fuels. For instance, both the Ford and Volkswagen companies now manufacture vehicles that will run on ethanol. In 1990, Brazil had more than 2.5 million

The Amazon rain forest of Brazil offers a large source of wood. Many people worry that Brazil will cut down too much of the rain forest, leading to the destruction of thousands of plant and animal species.

ethanol-powered vehicles on the road. In addition to utilizing plants from its rain forests, Brazil grows thousands of acres of crops especially for the production of alcohol fuel. In the United States, alcohol fuel is most commonly found in a product called gasohol, a mixture of ethanol and gasoline. Such mixtures can be used in most car and truck engines but are presently available at only a handful of service stations.

Companies in the United States mix alcohol fuel with gasoline to lessen some of the harmful effects of using pure methanol and ethanol. Although the alcohol fuels burn more cleanly than petroleum products, they release formaldehyde into the air. Formaldehyde is a chemical known to cause cancer. Methanol and ethanol also cause more wear on car engines and make cold engines harder to start. Engineers are working on ways to eliminate these drawbacks to alcohol fuels. They are confident that in time these, along with other fuels derived from liv-

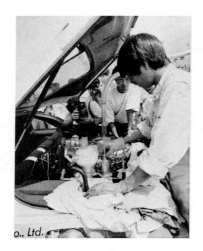

o., Ltd.

These Japanese students pump liquid hydrogen into the tank of a converted Nissan during a test run of the experimental car.

ing things, will significantly contribute to future energy production.

Hydrogen is another promising alternative fuel. Hydrogen is the most abundant element in nature. Hydrogen gas makes up 99 percent of the masses of stars like the sun. And every molecule of water in the earth's oceans, lakes, and rivers contains two atoms of hydrogen.

By using electrolysis to divide water molecules into atoms of hydrogen and oxygen, power plant operators can collect supplies of pure hydrogen gas. The hydrogen can then be burned as a fuel. Already, experimental hydrogen-powered vehicles are being tested. In West Germany, both the Mercedes Benz and BMW car companies have built experimental hydrogen-powered cars. In the 1980s, engineers in Provo, Utah, and Riverside, California, tested hydrogen-powered buses. A new experimental program for producing hydrogen cars began in California in 1990.

Advantages of hydrogen

There are several advantages to using hydrogen as a fuel. First, as mentioned, it is abundant. Hydrogen also burns the most cleanly of any known fuel. Such burning produces no air pollutants, not even carbon dioxide. The only exhausts produced by a hydrogen-powered vehicle are water vapor and some trace amounts of nitrogen oxide. Thus, burning hydrogen produces water, from which more hydrogen fuel can be extracted. This makes hydrogen fuel renewable and efficient.

There are also disadvantages to hydrogen fuel. The most serious problem is that hydrogen gas is highly flammable (liable to catch fire) and explosive. Therefore, it is dangerous to handle and transport. The hydrogen can be combined with metals called hydrides, which make it less flammable and therefore much safer to use. However, hydrides are heavy and seriously reduce fuel mileage in vehicles.

If these disadvantages can be overcome, millions of cars in the next century may run on hydrogen.

Another promising energy alternative being developed is the fuel cell. Fuel cells are now used in a limited capacity in utility plants and the space industry to produce electricity. Using a complicated atomic process, fuel cells convert hydrogen into electricity. Because this process does not rely on combustion or burning, it does not pollute the environment. The United States and Japan are still experimenting with this unique energy source. But for now, fuel cells are too costly and cannot compete with other, less expensive technology.

As new technological advances reshape the energy industry, fuel cells, hydrogen and the other renewable alternative fuels could potentially replace the fossil fuels. In addition, completely new alternative fuels and energy sources may be found that might alter the energy production industry in ways no one yet imagines.

Hydrogen gas is highly flammable, a point brought home by the fire that destroyed the famous Hindenburg *in 1937.*

8

Energy Conservation

EVERY SOURCE of energy has its disadvantages. Fossil fuels are limited and pollute the environment. Nuclear reactors generate radioactive wastes, and building hydroelectric plants requires flooding river valleys. To be effective, solar panels and reflectors must cover large tracts of land, and geothermal wells dredge up rubble from the earth's interior. Even clean-burning and nonpolluting hydrogen is explosive and dangerous to handle. And all of these alternatives are expensive to develop and utilize.

One way to minimize these disadvantages is to use less energy. When people use less energy, less energy needs to be produced. Generating energy is then not so costly and not so harmful to the environment. Using less energy does not have to mean learning to live with less comfort. It does not mean that people will have to turn down their heat and freeze in the winter or trade in their cars for bicycles and horses. Every year, vast amounts of energy are wasted because many people are careless about the way they use energy. People can use significantly less energy simply by learning to conserve energy better.

The conservation efforts initiated in 1973 have

(opposite page) Americans depend heavily on many energy sources. The importance of these is rarely clearer than when they suddenly come to a halt. Here, a power outage leaves New York City traffic hopelessly tangled.

demonstrated that energy conservation can play a major role in solving energy problems. Governments spent relatively little money on conservation, yet they saved a great deal of energy. For instance, in 1984, the U.S. government spent forty-four billion dollars on energy research and production. More than 53 percent of the money went to increasing the supply of fossil fuels. About 35 percent was spent on nuclear power, 5 percent on hydroelectric power, and 4 percent on all the other types of power combined. The government spent only 2 percent of the money trying to find ways of conserving energy. Yet the amount of energy saved in 1985 and 1986 was six times the amount of energy used by new sources of coal and nuclear power. Thus, conserving energy proved to be much more efficient than searching for more energy.

Experts across the United States agree that conservation efforts need to be greatly expanded. "We approach the energy problem with big plans," complains John Eells, Transportation Planning Coordinator for Marin County, California. "New electric

Because large amounts of heat energy may be lost in homes, many people line the walls and ceilings of their homes with several inches of insulation.

plants, more drilling for oil—always looking at supply, screaming 'we need more, we need more.' We need to focus on our demand. Focusing on supply assumes our present consumption can go on forever. It can't. Conservation is the area where we need to put our greatest efforts."

Many people make no effort to conserve energy because they think a single person or family cannot have a significant effect on the energy problem. They think energy conservation should start with the major industries. Large companies do use and waste a great deal of the energy produced in the world each day. But the truth is that individual citizens—all the homeowners, consumers, and drivers combined—use and waste a large portion of the world's energy. Therefore, by conserving energy in their everyday lives, people can make a major contribution to reducing the world's energy consumption.

Saving energy at home

Heating rooms and water consumes most of the energy used in homes. Experts say that people can conserve much of this energy by using common sense. For instance, when asleep in bed, people are covered by blankets. Therefore, the temperature of the house's interior does not need to be as high at night as it does in the daytime. By turning down their thermostats when sleeping, and also when they are away from home, people can save a great deal of energy.

Large amounts of heat energy are lost in homes that are poorly insulated. For instance, all walls and ceilings facing the outside should be lined with several inches of insulation. Some people are careful about this type of insulation but forget about heat loss through cracks around doors and windows. These should be caulked and weather-stripped.

Because heat rises, it collects near high ceilings, where it is wasted. Installing a fan in the ceiling

Water heaters and furnaces can be covered with special blankets to help keep heat from escaping.

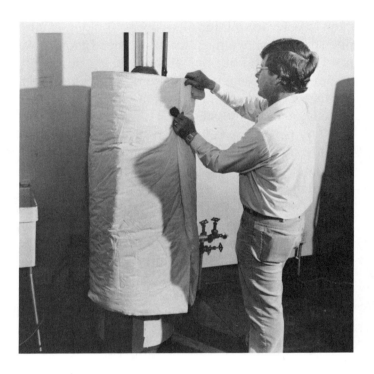

helps push warm air downward. Recirculating the air with the fan uses less energy than warming more air with the furnace. The furnace itself can contribute to heat loss if it is not operating efficiently. Experts estimate that as much as 30 to 50 percent of the energy produced by a furnace will be wasted if the device is not working properly. Yearly tune-ups by a heating company can eliminate this problem.

Heating water for showers, automatic dishwashers, and washing machines requires a lot of energy. Unfortunately, many people waste hot water. They take long showers and run their dishwashers unnecessarily. To use energy most efficiently, people should wait until their dishwashers and washing machines are full before running them. Also, 25 percent of the hot water used in an average house can be saved if people turn off the shower while soaping and turn it on again to rinse. They can save another 50 percent of the hot water by installing a special water-saving shower head. This device constricts the flow of water, while allowing water pressure and rinsing power to remain the same.

Conserving household electricity

Because it takes a great deal of energy to generate electricity, using electric appliances and devices wisely is one way people can make a significant contribution to energy conservation. Ideally, appliances that use a lot of electricity should be replaced by appliances that require less power to operate. For example, because an air conditioner uses much more electricity per hour than a fan, using the fan conserves energy. Similarly, high-wattage light bulbs use more energy than low-wattage bulbs. Therefore, in areas where bright lights are not needed, it makes more sense to use low-wattage bulbs.

Two light bulbs with the same wattage are not necessarily equally efficient. For instance, fluorescent lights often use three times less energy than

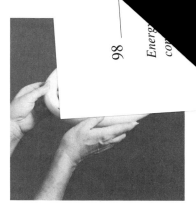

Flourescent lights, like this flourescent light ring, can help save energy. Converting a third of conventional household lights to flourescents can save on electricity costs.

Energy can be used more efficiently by running dishwashers only when they are full.

conventional incandescent bulbs of the same wattage. And some fluorescent lights last up to twenty times longer. Converting only one-third of the conventional lights in a home to fluorescents could save the home owner more than one hundred dollars a year in electricity costs.

Another device that often wastes electricity is the refrigerator. The American Council for an Energy-Efficient Economy estimates that refrigerators use 7 percent of the nation's electricity. According to the council, many older refrigerators are not well insulated and leak much of the cold air they produce. As the devices try to generate more cold air, they use excess amounts of power. Also, people often keep their refrigerators and freezers colder than is necessary, wasting as much as 25 percent of the energy the devices use. The council estimates that more efficient use of refrigerators could save the United States the amount of electricity generated by twenty-three large power plants.

The throw-away society

Another way people waste energy in their homes is by using large numbers of disposable products. The manufacture of every item in a typical home requires energy. Obviously then, an item that is used over and over is more energy efficient than an item used only once and thrown away. Yet Americans and people in most other industrialized countries use

People can save energy by recycling many products used for packaging, such as aluminum cans, glass, plastic, and paper products.

huge amounts of disposable products each day. For example, they use millions of disposable plastic diapers, the manufacture of which uses much more energy than does cleaning cloth diapers. The disposables are then carted away to landfills, where dealing with them requires the expenditure of still more energy.

People can save vast amounts of energy by recycling, or reusing, many of the products designed to be thrown away. For example, most of the disposable products used in the United States consist of various types of containers, wrapping, and packaging. As much as 75 percent of the glass, 50 percent of the paper, 40 percent of the aluminum, and 8 per-

More and more companies are setting up recycling stations where people can bring their glass, paper, and metal.

cent of the steel produced are used for the packaging of goods. All these products can be recycled. Glass bottles can be sterilized and reused. Even when the glass is broken, it can be melted down and used to make new bottles. Paper products can be recycled to make newsprint, books, cardboard, paper plates, and napkins.

Some large companies are already setting an example for individual consumers by establishing official recycling policies. Proctor and Gamble is making soap containers from recycled plastic, which can also be used as a building material for homes and businesses. In 1990, several McDonald's restaurants began asking their customers to throw plastic foam containers into special trash cans. The foam is collected and recycled. More and more trash landfills are setting up recycling stations where consumers can bring their separated glass, paper, and metal. Experts agree that if most American companies and consumers regularly practiced recycling, the demand for energy would significantly decrease.

Saving energy in transportation

Vehicles such as cars and trucks waste enormous amounts of energy. For instance, large cars require large engines, which in turn require large amounts of fuel. Some large cars get only ten to fifteen miles on a gallon of fuel, while smaller, more fuel efficient cars get twenty-five to forty miles on a gallon. Since many people buy large cars, a great deal of fuel is wasted. Another way vehicles waste energy is through unnecessary use. Often, people from the same neighborhood, even the same family, drive separate cars to the same destination. Thus, even though only one car is needed, two or three cars are used, burning fuel, consuming energy, and producing air pollution.

People can conserve energy by buying smaller, more fuel efficient cars. Some large automobile

manufacturers have already begun to produce cars that burn significantly less fuel. For example, the Toyota AXV, developed in the late 1980s, gets an average of ninety-eight miles to the gallon. By car-pooling, especially when commuting to work in cities, people can keep many unnecessary vehicles off the road. This saves fuel, reduces air pollution, which requires energy to clean up, and decreases the number of traffic jams.

Vehicle owners also can conserve energy by getting regular tune-ups. Old spark plugs and filters can reduce fuel efficiency. In addition, keeping the tires properly inflated saves fuel. Underinflated tires can waste as much as 5 percent of a vehicle's fuel.

Insurance company employees in Hartford, Connecticut board a company van that will take them home from work. Van and car pooling help conserve fuel and the expense.

What industry and business can do

Because industry and business account for much of the energy consumed in the United States, their conservation efforts can greatly affect the nation's total energy consumption. Energy-wise construction, insulation, heating, cooling, and lighting of commercial and government buildings can save a large percentage of the world's energy. Energy saving measures can benefit businesses as well as society. The World Bank spent $100,000 to make its lighting more energy efficient. This investment has saved them $500,000 in electricity costs every year! In partnership, governments and industry can research and develop more efficient means of converting energy and energy-efficient vehicles, appliances, and machinery. Researchers are discovering new processes for efficient energy use. Cogeneration is a good example.

Using waste heat

Converting one form of energy to another loses or wastes much of the energy as heat. Using this wasted heat as an energy source is called cogeneration. For example, some plants and factories pump wasted hot water to apartments and factories to heat rooms. Other waste heat can be used to heat the factory in which it is generated, or to generate electricity. Cogeneration facilities have been installed in businesses across the nation. Besides saving energy, cogeneration can save money for businesses and government agencies.

Saving energy for a better future

The availability of affordable energy is perhaps the most important physical factor in people's lives. Without such energy, civilization, as it exists in modern technical societies, would be impossible. If energy production ceased today, almost all the comforts and conveniences people take for granted would disappear. Many hours now used to pursue careers, hobbies, and entertainment would have to be devoted to basic survival. Thus, to a large extent, the amount of energy people have at their fingertips determines whether or not their lives will be comfortable and fulfilling.

In order to ensure sufficient supplies of affordable energy for humanity's future, people must deal with the problem of energy production in three ways. First, they must explore and develop all possible alternative energy sources. At the same time, they must learn to make existing sources more efficient and nonpolluting. Finally, people must practice better conservation so that the energy produced lasts longer. Whether or not human civilization flourishes in the future depends very much on how the people of today use and misuse energy.

Glossary

acid rain: Rain, hail, or snow containing high levels of sulfuric or nitric acids, formed by leaching sulfur dioxide and nitrogen oxides from the air.

advanced oil recovery technology: Techniques for recovering oil that cannot be pumped easily from wells.

atom: The smallest unit of an element.

bioenergy: Energy converted from sunlight and stored in the bodies of plants and animals in the form of hydrocarbons.

biogas: A mixture of methane and carbon dioxide produced by the breakdown of biomass.

biomass: Plant and animal products or wastes, such as animal dung, sawdust, leftover wood parts from lumber mills, and leaves and wood from the forest floor.

cogeneration: A system that recovers heat wasted during an energy conversion process and uses the waste heat as an energy source.

control rods: Rods that contain substances that capture nuclei without splitting. They control the number of neutrons flying through uranium fuel in a nuclear reactor.

deuterium: A heavy form of hydrogen.

efficiency: In converting energy, the percentage of the energy put in that is converted into the new form of energy.

electrolysis: The process that passes electricity through molecules, thereby separating them into atoms.

ethanol: A form of alcohol that can be burned in vehicles as a fuel. It may be made chemically from petroleum products, but it is more often made from plant material.

104

fission: Splitting atoms into two or more smaller atoms.

fossil fuels: Fuels made in the earth from the remains of ancient living things. They include coal, natural gas, and petroleum.

fuels: Substances that produce energy when their forms are changed, usually by burning.

fusion: Joining atoms to make a larger atom. Fusion energy is what keeps the sun burning.

generator: A device that converts the mechanical energy from a turbine into electricity.

geothermal energy: Naturally occuring heat inside the earth.

hydrocarbon: Carbohydrate molecule containing only hydrogen and carbon. These molecules occur in bodies of living or once-living organisms, or in substances made from their bodies.

hydroelectric power: Electricity made by the motion of water.

methanol: A form of alcohol that can replace gasoline and other fuels.

nonrenewable resources: Resources that exist in limited supplies and cannot be replaced.

renewable resources: Those resources that are constantly renewed, such as the sun, or those that can be replaced, such as trees.

strip mining: A method of mining coal by removing the surface of the land. It is used to mine coal lying near the earth's surface.

turbines: Machines used to turn generators to make electricity. They have revolving blades that are set in motion by the force of steam, water, or hot expanding gases.

Organizations to Contact

Alliance to Save Energy
1925 K St. NW, Suite 206
Washington, DC 20006
(202) 857-0666

Energy Information Administration
RM I-F-048
Washington, DC 20585
(202) 586-8800

Environmental Action Resource Service
P.O. Box 8
Laveta, CO 81055

National Center for Appropriate Technology
P.O. Box 2525
Butte, MT 59702
(800) 428-2525

Rocky Mountain Institute
1739 Snowmass Creek Rd.
Old Snowmass, CO 81654-9199
(303) 927-3128

Seventh Generation
10 Farrell St.
S. Burlington, VT 05403
(800) 456-1177

Suggestions for Further Reading

Annual Energy Outlook 1990. Energy Information Administration.

John H. Douglas, *The Future World of Energy.* New York: Franklin Watts, 1984.

Energy 90. Santa Monica, CA: Enterprise for Education, 1989.

50 Simple Things You Can Do to Save the Earth. Berkeley: Earthworks Press, 1989.

Jeffrey Hollander, *How to Make the World a Better Place.* New York: Quill, William Morrow, 1990.

International Energy Annual. Energy Information Administration, updated yearly.

Mark Lambert, *Future Sources of Energy.* New York: The Bookwright Press, 1986.

Robin McKie, *Science Frontiers: Energy.* New York: Hampstead Press, 1989.

Jane Werner Watson, *Alternate Energy Sources.* New York: Franklin Watts, 1979.

Index

7

About the Author

A former teacher, Barbara Keeler is now an educational consultant and an educational writer. In addition to writing textbooks in a number of subject areas, she has written newspaper articles about environmental issues.

Picture Credits